The Gay Bible

- **Rose Buchanan**

© 2014 by Rose Buchanan

All rights reserved.

ISBN # 978-1-312-87280-6

The tragedy that nearly took my life led me to the cross. The process to get there was excruciating! I'm obligated to share my story with the world... especially GLBT people. I grew up believing in a punishing god because that is what I was taught. Those teachings turned me away from seeking a personal relationship with God, Jesus and the Holy Spirit... or anything else associated with religion. The devastating events in my life eventually led me to the Spirit. I felt rejected by many. The path was very lonely until I started believing that god was not, is not, punishing me.

Luke 21:16 And ye shall be betrayed both by parents, and brethren, and kinsfolks, and friends; and some of you shall they cause to be put to death. (17) And ye shall be hated of all men for my name's sake. (18) But there shall not an hair of your head perish.

Jesus absolutely adores us! I hope all of you will find this truth if you don't already know it. I hope those of you wanting to die will discover this amazing love that will save your life. I know it's real. I've lived in the depths of hell, wanting to die. Now, I live in the light and am overwhelmed, at times, with gratitude for being alive. Join me, won't you?

I. JESUS DOESN'T DISCRIMINATE p.6-8

II. JESUS DISPUTES MOSES' LAW p.9-24

III. HUMAN INTERPRETATION p.25-37

IV. WHO R U 2 JUDGE? p.38-42

V. LOVE p.43-55

VI. GET PERSONAL p.56-69

VII. WHAT 2 BELIEVE p.70-79

VIII. REFERENCES p.80

I. Jesus loves gay, bisexual, lesbian and transgender people. It is written everywhere in the bible. I'll highlight some verses for you.

Galatians 3:26-28 For ye are all the children of God by faith in Christ Jesus. (27) For as many of you as have been baptized into Christ have put on Christ. (28) There is neither Jew nor Greek, there is neither bond nor free, there is neither male nor female: for ye are all one in Christ Jesus.

Jesus doesn't discriminate against GLBT's, homophobes do. Jesus was crucified by phobic bullies. He knows exactly what we are going through. He hung on the cross for being different. He was meek, peaceful, loving and healing. He was considered an outcast. As a male, he seemed effeminate.

We, the GLBT's, are the people Jesus came to help and represent. I read some truths Jesus brought in the "King James" version of the New Testament. I will point out the verses where God says that human interpretations got the message wrong. It's about love, not punishment. Jesus will dispute those points and make the corrections. I will show you the good news that homophobes try to ignore.

1 John 4:20 If a man say, I love God, and hateth his brother, he is a liar: for he that loveth not his brother who he hath seen, how can he love God whom he hath not seen?

Some people try to use the bible to condone their hatred. They even go so far as to say that they are doing God's work by their vengeful actions.

John 16:2 & 3 Jesus said, "They shall put you out of the synagogues: yea, the time cometh, that whosoever killeth you will think that he doeth God service. And these things will they do unto you because they have not known the Father, nor me."

Jesus confirms that homophobes do not know Him or God, the Father, when they do such hateful acts towards GLBT people.

1 John 3:15 Whosoever hateth his brother is a murderer; and ye know that no murderer hath eternal life abiding in him.

John 15:18 Jesus said, "If the world hateth you, ye know that it hated me before it hated you.

Remember, Jesus was crucified by the same mentality that spews hatred against gays today. The scribes and Pharisees persecuted Jesus because he spoke against Moses' law. He spoke of strange things such as love all, help the needy, feed the poor, and take care of the sick. He was not married and had no children. He got close and personal with men and women in order to heal them, even though he didn't have to.

II. Some people consider themselves Christians. A Christian is supposed to mean you are a follower of Christ Jesus. Many of those people continue to follow the Old Testament, which is before Christ. Jesus brought the New Testament to show the errors and faults with Moses' law in the Old Testament.

John 1:17 For the law was given by Moses but grace and truth came by Jesus Christ.

That is a huge statement showing that Moses' laws and his interpretations are not exactly what God had intended. Here are some more indications:

Hebrews 3:3 For this man was counted worthy of more glory than Moses, in as much as he who hath builded the house has more honour than the house.

This verse points out that Jesus is above all, including Moses.

Hebrews 8:7 For if the first covenant had been faultless then should no place have been sought for the second.

God says the first covenant, the Old Testament, has faults; otherwise, there would have been no reason and need for Jesus to bring the second.

Hebrews 8:13 In that he saith, A new covenant he hath made the first old. Now that which decayeth and waxeth old is ready to vanish away.

This clearly states the Old Testament needs to be put away... vanish! The New Testament shows us better ways to live. Homophobes use the errors in Moses' law to bash gay people. There are several verses in the bible used to discriminate against GLBT's.

Leviticus 18:22 Thou shalt not lie with mankind as with woman kind: it is abomination.

Two verses prior to this one, the author specifies "carnally" to imply sexually lying together. So, the implication is not about sex in Lev. 18:22, but is in Leviticus 18:20. It reads: Moreover thou shalt not lie carnally with thy neighbor's wife, to defile thyself with her.

Of course, some people assume laying together automatically means having sex. The author made specific mention of carnally in one verse, but not the other. Another point is the definition of abomination. It means to hate. A thing hated or despised. Many things were considered abomination. It made no difference if it's being too proud, lying with beasts, (don't let your dog or cat curl up next to you!), adultery, seeing your mother or father naked, or being near a woman during her menstrual cycle. All these things and more were considered abomination, according to the Old Testament.

Leviticus 18:6 – 23 lists many abominations. Leviticus 20:9, cursing your father or mother shall put you to death. Proverbs 11:1 A false balance is abomination to the Lord: but a just weight is his delight. Proverbs 16:5 Everyone that is proud in heart is an abomination to the Lord though hand join in hand, he shall not be unpunished. Luke 16:15 And he said unto them, "Ye are they which justify yourselves before man: but God knoweth your heart: for that which is highly esteemed among men is abomination in the sight of God.

Of course, homophobes are the ones that try to make one verse stand out over any other of these abominations. Moses' interpretations of God's words had a lot of hatred and punishment. Maybe that is why God sent Jesus to correct these erroneous interpretations.

There are two other verses that people like to use against homosexuality.

Romans 1:26 and 27. For this cause God gave them up unto vile affections: for even the women did change the natural use into that which is against nature. (27) And likewise also the men, leaving their natural use of the women burned in their lust one towards another.

These verses sound similar to the homophobic rhetoric we hear today about what's natural. It's just more human interpretation of what God thought and did.

The next couple verses after Romans 1:27, list other actions ranging from boasting to murder, including being disobedient to parents as being worthy of death. Then he says but who are you to judge? Romans 2:1 Therefore thou art inexcusable O man, whosoever thou art that judgest: for wherein thou judgest another, thou condemnest thyself; for thou that judgest doest the same things.

This is how we know that those protesting the loudest against gays are the closet cases. Those that protest are just as gay, but trying to mask it due to some of society's hatred.

The next verse I bring up because the word "effeminate" is changed to "homosexual" in the "New Living Translation" bible. The two words do not mean the same thing. The authors or translators of that bible inserted the wrong word. Maybe that was done because the word homosexual is nowhere in the other bibles; and homophobes want to get it in there somewhere for future generations to read without questioning its validity.

1 Corinthians 6: 9-11 Know ye not that the unrighteous shall not inherit the kingdom of God? Be not deceived: neither fornicators, nor idolaters, nor adulterers, nor effeminate, nor abusers of themselves with mankind, (10) nor thieves, nor covetous, nor drunkards, nor revilers, nor extortioners, shall inherit the kingdom of God. (11) And such were some of you: but ye are washed, but ye are sanctified, but ye are justified in the name of the Lord Jesus, and by the Spirit of our God.

The word effeminate means 'having feminine qualities untypical of a man; not manly in appearance or manner'. The word homosexual means 'characterized by a tendency to direct sexual desire towards another of the same sex'. These are completely different words with distinctly different meanings. They are not interchangeable. The "New Living Translation" of the bible needs to be exposed for trying to perpetuate homophobia. I tell all the people that I know about this. I spread the word to throw out that version or just not use it as reliable. If that is their interpretation on those two words and by definition wrong, what else is misinterpreted? I came to that section in that bible and threw it out after that.

The other big controversial reference to homosexuality in the bible that people try to use against GLBT people is the destruction of Sodom and Gomorrah in Genesis 19. I have read a couple interpretations about the reasons for the destruction. One very good point brought up is that being unkind and inhospitable toward strangers is a huge sin back in the day. It still is in the Bible belt. I have plenty of kin in the south and know the phrase 'southern hospitality' to be very real and a big deal. These strangers in Genesis 19 happened to be God's angels that were treated unkind. That is one of the reasons to destroy the city.

Another huge problem with Sodom and Gomorrah gets pointed out several chapters prior to Genesis 19. This is why reading chapters and verses in proper order are important. People will pick one verse and pull it out of context and use it to bash others. The real wickedness of the men in Sodom and Gomorrah was from Noah's son, Ham, seeing Noah naked while Noah was drunk in his tent. It is written in Genesis 9:18 to explain who is who. Ham's son is Canaan. After Ham saw Noah naked, Noah cursed Canaan, his grandson, because of Ham's sin. That's in Genesis 9:25. Then it goes on to explain the family tree of each son. In Genesis 10:19 and 20, the borders of the Canaanites are explained. Sodom and Gomorrah are part of that territory. The territories and tongues spoken are named after the people and their family. So, Canaanites are of Canaan, which includes Sodom and Gomorrah. Anything of Canaan is cursed due to Ham seeing his father, Noah, naked. THAT is the abomination!

The wickedness of the men, Genesis 13:13, in Sodom and Gomorrah is due to Noah's curse. It is the only written explanation leading up to the destruction in Genesis 19. Then these wicked men were being unkind and inhospitable to God's angels. The abomination from seeing your father naked is brought up in Leviticus 18:6 and 20:11 and is punishable by death. This is the real sin of the men and why they are considered wicked... a curse from Noah.

Also written in Genesis 19, with the destruction of Sodom and Gomorrah, is incest and pimping. In Genesis 19:8, Lot offers his daughters to the strangers to do what they want to them. In Genesis 19:30-38, Lot and his daughters have sex and conceive babies. Each daughter gets Lot drunk, has sex, conceives and has a baby... by their father! All of that is over looked to say the destruction must be about homosexuality. Nowhere does is read that. Only homophobic minds would create lies like that to pass along for years. People just believe it without investigating. I knew in my heart that it couldn't really say or mean that with such a loving God that I know! So, I have taken the time and effort to read to seek the truth. And there it is. Check for yourself with this information I provided.

These are the verses from the entire bible that homophobes use to continue the spread of hatred and inequality. Jesus carries a different message. His is one of LOVE! Jesus disputes Moses' law to prove the errors of the Old Testament where the traditions of homophobic family values come from.

Jesus came to change the "traditions" and "historic" ways of Moses' law according to Acts 6:14; "For we have heard him say that this Jesus of Nazareth shall destroy this place and shall change the customs which Moses delivered us."

Moses' interpretation is not what God had intended. These interpretations are the traditions that homophobes try to use to justify their fears through their hate. Traditions based on fear, discrimination and exclusion are not what God's laws are about. Jesus talks about being born a certain way that old rules do not apply.

Matthew 19: 8-12 He saith unto them, Moses because of the hardness of your hearts suffered you to put away your wives:

but from the beginning it was not so. (9) And I say unto you, Whosoever shall put away his wife, except it be for fornication, and shall marry another, committeth adultery: and whoso marrieth her which is put away doth commit adultery. (10) His disciples say unto him, If the case of the man be so with his wife, it is not good to marry. (11) But he said unto them, All men cannot receive this saying, save they to whom it is given. (12) For there are some eunuchs, which were so born from their mother's womb: and there are some eunuchs, which were made eunuchs of men: and there be eunuchs which have made themselves eunuchs for the kingdom of heaven's sake. He that is able to receive it, let him receive it.

Eunuchs are men that don't have sex with women for various reasons. Some are born that way… GAY!!! So, Jesus said if the rules don't apply to some, let it be for those it does apply. THERE IT IS! Jesus points out that Moses' traditions aren't right for all people.

Acts 13:39 And by him all that believe are justified from all things from which ye could not be justified by the law of Moses.

Jesus is here to save us from the errors in Moses' interpretations of God's words.

Romans 3:28 Therefore we conclude that a man is justified by faith without the deeds of the law.

Romans5:1 Therefore being justified by faith, we have peace with God through our Lord Jesus Christ.

Romans 7:6 But now we are delivered from the law, that being dead wherein we were held; that we should serve in newness of Spirit, and not in the oldness of the letter.

We are delivered from the errors and faults of Moses' law through the Spirit of Christ Jesus. The letter of the law does not over rule the Spirit of LOVE, which is Jesus. It's all about the Love!!!

The Pharisees were constantly trying to tell Jesus that their way was right because it was according to Moses' law. It's all they knew to be "right". It was all they knew to become their traditions. Jesus said that it's not the way God intended, though.

Acts 15:5-9 But there rose up certain of the sect of the Pharisees which believed, saying that it was needful to circumcise them, and to command them to keep the law of Moses. (6) And the apostles and elders came together for to consider this matter. (7) And when there had been much disputing, Peter rose up, and said unto them, men and brothers, ye know how that a good while ago God made choice among us, that the Gentiles by my mouth should hear the word of the gospel and believe. (8) And God, which knoweth the hearts bare them witness, giving them the Holy Ghost, even as he did unto us; (9) And put no difference between us and them, purifying their hearts by faith.

Another great example showing that the Pharisees were certain their way was the only way and "right" because it was according to Moses' law. Jesus said that it's not the TRUTH. It's what's in your heart that matters… and if that's love, it's right. Also, circumcision was a huge issue and a covenant with God… a must according to Moses' law. Jesus said it doesn't matter.

In this next example, Jesus not only disputes Moses' law, but clearly states that every human being needs to check their own conscience and actions. Everyone should live according to his own conscience with God and not judge anyone else.

John 8:4-11 They say unto him, Master, this woman was taken in adultery, in the very act. (5) Now Moses in the law commanded us, that such should be stoned: but what sayest thou? (6) This they said, tempting him, that they might have to accuse him. But Jesus stooped down and with his finger wrote on the ground, as though he heard them not. (7) So when they continued asking him, he lifted up himself and said unto them, "He that is without sin among you, let him first cast a stone at her." (8) And again he stooped down and wrote on the ground. (9) And they which heard it, being convicted by their own conscience, went out one by one beginning at the eldest, even unto the last: and Jesus was left alone, and the woman standing in the midst. (10) When Jesus lifted up himself and saw none but the woman, he said unto her, "Woman, where are those thine accusers? Hath no man condemned thee?" (11) She said, No man, Lord. And Jesus said unto her, "Neither do I condemn thee: go, and sin no more."

These verses talk about Moses law commanding to stone her for adultery. According to Moses' law in Leviticus 20:10, adultery was a death sentence. Jesus said WRONG! Everyone checks yourself and own life and not judge others. All people have done things wrong; so, no one has the right to judge another. Jesus has the power to judge, but doesn't.

Acts 10:28 And he said unto them, ye know how it is an unlawful thing for a man that is a Jew to keep company or come unto one of another nation; but God hath shewed me that I should not call any man common or unclean.

Romans 14:14 I know that I am persuaded by the Lord Jesus that there is nothing unclean of itself: but to him that esteemeth anything to be unclean, to him it is unclean.

So, the homophobes can quit claiming God says homosexuality is wrong. We know that it is hatred from humans, not God.

Colossians 2:14 Blotting out the handwriting of ordinances that was against us, while was contrary to us, and took it out of the way, nailing it to his cross.

WOW!!! Jesus took all the old discriminating traditions and historic ways of Moses' that came from fear and ignorance and nailed it to his cross. He covered everything and washes us clean. His blood sets us free… sets the captives free. Jesus carries the message of Love, not hate.

III. All the chapters in the bible are from human interpretations of God's words. That means there are flaws, since humans are imperfect. Interpretation of events is unique to the individual. Some of the people in the bible were quite frightened by the strange happenings that they witnessed. So, their interpretations were fear based. Others were amazed. Some of their interpretations were based on being awestruck, perhaps. I know mine is based on amazement, too. Someone writing their view based on fear is going to be very different than someone's based on wonderment.

In Mark 5:1-20, the story is about devils being in a man. He was tormented by them. The man saw Jesus and asked him for help. Jesus told the devils to get out of the man. There were some pigs nearby. The devils asked if they could go into the pigs. Jesus let them do so. The pigs went crazy, running into the sea and they drowned. The people watching all of this were fearful. They asked Jesus to leave. The man that Jesus saved asked if he could go with Jesus. Jesus said that he should go tell others of his experience of being saved.

These are contrasting views of the same event by different people. Some were fear based. Others were amazed and praised Jesus.

In Mark 5: 25-34, a woman is sick and touches Jesus' garment in order to be healed. He asked who touched him. She was hesitant to tell but then confessed it was her. Jesus said that it is her belief that heals and makes her whole; healing is not from touching him. He said that our belief is what will heal or destroy us. If we believe in love, tolerance, kindness, mercy, and peace, we will have those things in our lives. We will be peaceful within our own skin. If people believe in discrimination and hatred, their lives will be destructive and chaotic. Hatred is fear. Fear is lack of faith. It is unhealthy to the mind and heart. What we believe is very powerful and guides our lives.

Matthew 18:6 But whose shall offend one of these little ones which believes in me, it were better for him that a millstone were hanged about his neck and that he were drowned in the depth of the sea.

Jesus gets angry at injustices. He says you'd be better off dead than to mess with one of God's kids. He is showing an appropriate reaction to someone being offensive to one of his. Jesus stands for protection of the oppressed.

In John 6:60-66, even Jesus' disciples don't always believe what they are seeing. These are the ones that Jesus handpicked. Jesus knows there is doubt and tells them that only those that believe can walk with him. Some of them walked with him and some didn't. They walked away. Even though Jesus selected these people, they are still imperfect human beings. They witnessed his miracles and still could not believe. They walked away. Jesus didn't punish them. He just continued on his path. He lets people go by their own conscience, with or without him.

John 14:10 Believest thou not that I am in the Father, and the Father in me? The words that I speak unto you I speak not of myself: but the Father that dwelleth in me, he doeth the works.

These people that Jesus picked have their stories in the bible, even though they doubted. Many of them were so accustomed to the traditions of Moses' law that they couldn't change their way of seeing things even being told and shown by Jesus Christ. I think the extreme homophobes are like that, too. Even with Jesus' message of love all, they still hate. Their fears run their life instead of Jesus' love running their hearts.

In Acts 10, Peter was hungry, went into a trance and was told to rise, kill and eat. He said that he had never eaten anything common or unclean. The voice spoke to him again saying what God has cleaned is not common. This was said three times. Peter doubted though. While Peter thought on the vision, the Spirit said to him that three men sought him; "arise and go with them doubting nothing, for I have sent them."

It was very hard for Peter to believe a different way after being taught never to eat certain things. The voice told him to go ahead and eat. He didn't know how to interpret it. The Spirit told him to go ahead because God cleansed it. A Spirit telling him different than his traditions according to Moses' law created doubts as to what is right. He had ingrained ways in his belief system that it was not alright to do something. Then a new way and new idea came along.

Most homophobic people that claim they are Christian come from believing the old traditional lies. It is ingrained so deeply that their minds close shut at anything different and new that might break traditions.

Romans 8:18 For I reckon that the sufferings of this present time are not worthy to be compared with the glory which shall be revealed in us.

Based on my personal experience as a believer in Jesus Christ, God's glory is much more powerful than the human struggles I have faced. That's how and why I'm writing this. The struggles only strengthen my faith and relationship with Jesus, when I turned to him. I believe that is why the homophobes want us to believe that God hates us; so we won't get plugged into the power available through Jesus' love. That love will make us more powerful in Spirit and unbreakable in our quest for equality! God, Jesus and the Holy Spirit are for us, not against us!!! I know this from personal experience, not just from reading the bible.

1 Corinthians 1:27-28 But God has chosen the foolish things of this world to confound the wise; and God has chosen the weak things of the world to confound the things which are mighty; (28) And base things of the world, and things which are despised, hath God chosen, yea and things which are not, to bring to nought things that are.

These are very clear verses that God doesn't hate GBLT's. We are chosen by God because we are despised by homophobes hiding behind Jesus' name. We are sooo loved by Jesus!

1 Corinthians 7:1 (of celibacy and marriage) Now concerning the things where of ye wrote unto me: It is good for a man not to touch a woman.

This verse can easily be used as proof that gay is the right way for all people. It's a matter of personal interpretation. If you are heterosexual, it's a different interpretation than if you are gay.

Genesis 3:16 Unto the woman he said, I will greatly multiply thy sorrow and thy conception; in sorrow thou shalt bring forth children; and thy desire shall be to thy husband, and he shall rule over thee.

This verse has to be my favorite for pointing out the punishment God gave Eve according to Moses' interpretation. This speaks volumes that it is a punishment for a woman to get married to a man and have children. Again, proof that gay is the way. These are the verses the homophobes don't want known because it validates that the straight life is a punishment for homosexuals.

1 Corinthians 7:6 and 7 But I speak this by permission, and not of commandment. (7) For I would that all men were even as I myself. But every man hath his proper gift of God, one after this manner, and another after that.

The author of this book, Paul, admits what he writes is not commandments from God, but his opinions. All of the authors in the bible wrote their interpretations and personal opinions. The same as I am doing. Mine is based on my personal experiences with my relationship with Jesus Christ. I am a human being sharing my personal interpretations of God's words. The traditions of Moses' law were fully believed, maybe, but Jesus came to say some of them are wrong. They are not accurate interpretations of God's words… not even close to God's message of Love.

1 Corinthians 7:12 (advise to those married) But to the rest speak I, not the Lord…

Again, another example of Paul admitting that these are his interpretations; they are not God's words.

1 Corinthians 7:25 (advise to those unmarried) Now concerning virgins I have no commandment of the Lord: yet I give my judgement as one that hath obtained mercy of the Lord to be faithful.

He has NO COMMANDMENT FROM GOD, Paul admits. Each person must deal with their own conscience and their relationship with God and others.

Philemon 1:1 Paul, a prisoner of Jesus Christ…

If Paul, the author of many chapters in the bible, felt like a prisoner of Jesus Christ, he would probably have a different view as a free man. I'm just pointing out the different perspectives people write through. Those are interesting choices of words coming from a man writing in the bible. Jesus is supposed to set us free, not make us feel like a prisoner.

The book of Revelations has some extreme examples of opposite interpretations compared to the rest of the New Testament. It shows more discrepancies in the bible. This next chapter is written by John while he is in exile.

Revelations 2:6 But this thou hast, that thou hatest the deeds of the Nicolai tans, which I also hate.

John is claiming that Jesus said he hates something. This contradicts all of Jesus' teachings of love and peace and tolerance. The next couple of verses show the same discrepancy.

Revelations 2:15 …which I hate …

Again, Jesus supposedly said he hates something.

Revelations 2:23 And I will kill her children…

WOW! Now this is implying that Jesus said he'd kill children after the rest of the bible discusses his love and protection of children. These are BIG discrepancies and contradictions.

Revelations 11:8 And their dead bodies shall lie in the street of the great city, which spiritually is called Sodom and Egypt where also our Lord was crucified.

This verse indicates that Sodom was a spiritual place. It shows the misinterpretation of the destruction. It also reinforces that my assessment of the destruction is more accurate than that of homophobes… or anyone else believing the destruction was due to homosexuality. Anytime a child of God is murdered, it is another crucifixion of Christ, since He is in all of us.

It is easy to see the genuine parts in the bible from the discrepancies. I would not have known that had I not read the "King James" version of the bible for myself. Most people don't want to read and have not read the bible. They depend on others for their information. There are so many bad and hateful interpretations out in society. The sad fact is that people then believe these erroneous opinions based on lack of knowledge. Depending completely on another person's interpretation of such important matters is dangerous. This is how all these lies about homosexuality have stuck with so many generations. This is why I decided to do my own research and write about it. I want to give a condensed version of the good points and point out that there are only a couple verses that all homophobes try to bash GLBT people; and those are taken out of context. I provide proof that Jesus LOVES gay, lesbian, bi-sexual and transgender people.

Romans 5:8 But God commandeth his love towards us, in that, while we were yet sinners, Christ died for us.

We are all considered "sinners". I don't care for that word so I replace it with 'humans that make mistakes'. Jesus was supposed to be the only human form without sin. The rest of us are all equally human with imperfections. That means there are no bragging rights or superiority rights. We can't earn grace. It is given to us the moment we believe in Jesus Christ. He died on the cross so that we may know we are loved just as we are…

imperfect human beings. Once we feel that love, we will want to do better because of what He did for us. Jesus says we are holy and worthy just as we are. Being gay doesn't change that.

Romans 3:22-24 and 27 Even the righteousness of God which is by faith of Jesus Christ unto all and upon all them that believe: for there is no difference: (23) For all have sinned and come short of the glory of God; (24) Being justified freely by his grace through the redemption that is in Christ Jesus. (27) Where is the boasting then? It is excluded. By what law? Of works? Nay: but by the law of faith.

Jesus doesn't discriminate against GLBT people; homophobes do! People passing judgement based on long standing lies and fears are the problems in our society. Jesus talks a lot about judgement.

IV.   Matthew 7:1 Judge not that ye be not judged.

One of the biggest problems on our planet is judging each other to the negative extreme. Homophobes are judging GLBT's based on lack of knowledge… ignorance.

Luke 6:37 Judge not, and ye shall not be judged: condemn not, and ye shall not be condemned: forgive, and ye shall be forgiven.

Yes… if only in our society. Everything would be so much better for everyone.

John 5:22 For the Father judgeth no man but hath committed all judgement unto the Son.

John 8:15-18 (Jesus) Ye judge after the flesh: I judge no man. (16) And yet if I judge, my judgement is true: for I am not alone, but I and the Father that sent me. (17) It is also written in your law, that the testimony of two men is true. (18) I am one that bear witness of myself, and the Father that sent me beareth witness of me.

Jesus has the power from God to judge but does not. He again disputes Moses' law about testimony of two. These verses also help to completely tear apart the theory of a punishing God.

Romans 2:14, 15, 16 For when the gentiles which have not the law do by nature the things contained in the law, these, having not the law, are a law unto themselves. (15) Which shew the work of the law written in their hearts, their conscience also bearing witness and their thoughts the meanwhile accusing or else excusing one another. (16) In the day when God shall judge the secrets of men by Jesus Christ according to my gospel.

These verses point out that GLBT people do what is natural; and that's not what's natural for heterosexuals. It may not be written in the laws, yet, but it is written in people's hearts and God knows our hearts!

Romans 5:18 Therefore as by the offense of one judgement came upon all men to condemnation; even so by the righteousness of one the free gift came upon all men unto justification of life.

According to the bible, what Adam (the straight guy) did condemned us all. What Jesus (the effeminate guy) did, freed us all… all that believe in His teachings. Well, that is the way it is supposed to be. Jesus came to tell us the good news and free us from Moses' interpretations of condemnation. Homophobes want to keep us stuck in condemnation and not be freed by Jesus' Love.

Romans 14:4, 5 Who art thou that judgest another man's servant? To his own master he standeth or falleth. Yea, he shall be holden up: for God is able to make him stand. (5) One man esteemeth one day above another: Another esteemeth every day alike. Let every man be fully persuaded in his own mind.

Mind your own business and check your own conscience with your interpretation of your God. People that are stuck in their beliefs that homosexuality is wrong should keep it to themselves instead of trying to force those beliefs onto the world. GLBT people only want the actions of hate and discrimination to change. Homophobes can keep their beliefs if they so choose, just change the hateful behavior.

Romans 14:10, 12, 13 But why dost thou judge thy brother? Or why dost thou set at naught thy brother? For we shall all stand before the judgement seat of Christ. (12) So then every one of us shall give account of himself to God. (13) Let us not therefore judge one another any more: but judge this rather that no man put a stumbling block or an occasion to fall in his brother's way.

We are supposed to help each other up, not shove each other to the ground to get ahead.

1 Corinthians 6:2 Do ye not know that the saints shall judge the world? If the world shall be judged by you, are ye unworthy to judge the smallest matters?

Homophobes are not qualified to judge gay, lesbian, bi-sexual or transgender people.

James 4:12 There is one lawgiver, who is able to save and to destroy: who art thou that judgest another?

Homophobes are not qualified to judge the hearts, lives, laws or anything else regarding GLBT people. No one is supposed to be tearing down anyone. We are supposed to love each other. That is Jesus' message. It's all about the love!

V. Jesus tells us the most important thing in life is love. He gives us only two commandments to live by, which supersedes everything.

Matthew 22:37-40 Jesus said unto him, "Thou shalt love the Lord thy God with all thy heart, and with all thy soul, and with all thy mind, (38) This is the first and greatest commandment (39) And the second is like unto it, thou shalt love thy neighbor as thyself. (40) On these two commandments hang all the law and the prophets.

WOW! Jesus makes it clear and simple. Hating, discriminating and the like are against God's law of Love! Jesus overrules any other old ideas.

Luke 4:18 (Jesus) The Spirit of the Lord is upon me, because he hath anointed me to preach the gospel to the poor; he hath sent me to heal the brokenhearted, to preach deliverance to the captives, and recovering sight to the blind, to set at liberty them that are bruised.

I didn't read anything in there about hate and keep people from loving each other. It's about healing and freedom. The phrase 'to set at liberty' means the quality or state of being free; powers to do as one pleases.

Luke 6:22, 23 (Jesus) Blessed are ye, when men shall hate you, and when they shall separate you from their company, and shall reproach you, and cast out your name as evil, for the son of man's sake. (23) Rejoice ye in that day and leap for joy: for behold, your reward is great in heaven: for in the like manner did their father's unto the prophets.

The phobic mentality that crucified Jesus for his differences, are the same type that are crucifying gay, lesbian, bi-sexual and transgender people. We can celebrate that Jesus knows what we are going through. We can claim the power of Jesus to help us get through anything. Jesus Christ is always available to those that seek Him.

Luke 10:17-20 And the 70 returned again with joy saying, Lord, even the devils are subject unto us through thy name. (18) And he said unto them, I beheld Satan as lightning fall from heaven. (19) Behold, I give unto you power to tread on serpents and scorpions, and over all the power of the enemy: and nothing shall by any means hurt you. (20) Not withstand in this rejoice not, that the spirits are subject unto you; but rather rejoice, because your names are written in heaven.

I absolutely love these verses because of their reality in my life. I went through some tremendous events that proved these true. Through my faith in Jesus Christ, I survived a stampede of devils to share this message with all of you. I'll provide more details in my next writings.

John 3:16-19 For that God so loved the world that he gave his only begotten son that whosoever believeth in him should not perish but have everlasting life. (17) For God sent not his son into the world to condemn the world; but that the world through him might be saved. (18) He that believeth on him is not condemned:

but he that believeth not is condemned already because he hath not believed in the name of the only begotten son of God. (19) And this is the condemnation, that light is come into the world and men loved darkness rather than light because their deeds were evil.

God absolutely loves us! He sent Jesus to show us the way of peace and love; tolerance, healing and freedom from condemnation. Homophobes want us to believe we are hated and condemned by God so we won't seek the light. They want us to stay in darkness with their hatred. Just step into the light and love of Jesus and you'll grow beyond all the darkness of hate.

John 6:37-38, 40 (Jesus) All that the Father giveth me shall come to me; and him that cometh to me I will in no wise cast out. (38) For I came down from heaven, not to do mine own will, but the will of him that sent me. (40) And this is the will of him that sent me, that every one which seeth the son, and believeth on him, may have everlasting life: and I will rise him up at the last day.

Jesus casts no one out that wants Him and believes in Him.

John 14:12 (Jesus) Verily, verily, I say unto you, he that believeth on me, the works that I do shall he do also; and greater works than these shall he do; because I go unto my Father.

Jesus Christ gives us power to heal and help each other; not to destroy and hate. This is a pretty powerful statement in that we can do greater works than Jesus when we follow His path. His ways are simple and direct... peace and love.

Romans 8:35-39 Who shall separate us from the love of Christ? shall tribulation, or distress, or persecution, or famine, or nakedness, or peril, or sword? (36) As it is written, for thy sake we are killed all the day long; we are accounted as sheep for the slaughter. (37) Nay, in all these things we are more than conquerors through him that loved us. (38) For I am persuaded that neither death, nor life, nor angels, nor principalities, nor powers, nor things present, nor things to come, (39) Nor height, nor depth, nor any other creature shall be able to separate us from the love of God, which is in Christ Jesus our Lord.

Please don't let homophobes separate you from God's beautifully powerful Love. God is in love with us. You should try a love affair with Christ! It's amazing… the greatest lover I've ever had, or ever will!!!

Romans 13:8-10 Owe no man anything, but to love one another: for he that loveth another hath fulfilled the law. (9) For this, thou shalt not commit adultery, thou shalt not kill, thou shalt not steal, thou shalt not bear false witness, thou shalt not covet; and if there be any other commandment, it is briefly comprehended in this saying, namely, Thou shalt love thy neighbor as thyself. (10) Love worketh no ill to his neighbor: therefore love is the fulfilling of the law.

Jesus says that if you can't remember all the "THOU SHALL NOT's", just remember to LOVE GOD, self and others. That keeps it simple and covers everything.

Galatians 1:15 and 16 But when it pleased God, who separated me from my mother's womb, and called me by his grace, (16) To reveal his son in me…

God made us the way we are inside and out. Gay is o.k.! Christ is in us… we are HOLY!

Galatians 6:2 Bear ye one another's burdens, and so fulfill the law of Christ.

Ephesians 2:4-10 But God, who is rich in mercy, for his great love where with he loved us, (5) Even when we were dead in sins, hath quickened us together with Christ, (by grace ye are saved;) (6) And hath raised us up together, and made us sit together in heavenly places in Christ Jesus: (7) That in the ages to come he might shew the exceeding riches of his grace in his kindness toward us through Christ Jesus. (8) For by grace are ye saved through faith: and that not of yourselves: it is the gift of God: (9) Not of works, lest any man should boast. (10) For we are his workmanship, created in Christ Jesus unto good works, which God hath before ordained that we should walk in them.

We are born the way we are… God's workmanship. We are holy and loved, not because of what we do, but because of what He did for us. No one is superior to anyone else. We are equal in Christ!

Ephesians 4:32 And be ye kind one to another, tenderhearted, forgiving one another, even as God for Christ's sake hath forgiven you.

It didn't mention to hate and discriminate.

Ephesians 5:1 and 2 Be ye therefore followers of God, as dear children: And walk in love, as Christ also hath loved us, and hath given himself for us an offering and a sacrifice to God for a sweet smelling savour.

We are God's kids made with love!

2 Timothy 1:7 For God hath not given us the spirit of fear; but power, and love, and of a sound mind.

Phobia is fear. God didn't put homophobia in people, society did. The fearful interpretations in the Old Testament set up traditions based on hate, not love.

Titus 2:11 For the grace of God that bringeth salvation hath appeared to all men.

Some of us accept this grace when we believe and follow Jesus' path. Others don't. But it is for all people, not just a select few. Homophobes want us to think it's not for us; as if God left us out. God adores us!!!

1 Peter 1:22 Seeing ye have purified your souls in obeying the truth through the Spirit unto unfeigned love of the brethren, see that ye love one another with a pure heart fervently.

The truth of the Spirit is Love… an all inclusive, never exclusive Love. When we build a personal relationship with Jesus, this truth is revealed.

1 Peter 2:24 Who his own self bare our sins in his own body on the tree, that we, being dead to sins, should live unto righteousness: by whose stripes ye were healed.

Jesus' path of Love, mercy and kindness was shown to us so we could know how much we are loved. We were told the lies of a punishing God from old ideas based on fear. We can be healed by accepting Jesus' love and rejecting Moses' laws of punishment.

1 Peter 3:8 Finally, be ye all of one mind, having compassion one of another, love as brethren, be pitiful, be courteous.

We are one in love, separated by hate.

1 Peter 3:15 But sanctify the Lord God in your hearts: and be ready always to give an answer to every man that asketh you a reason of the hope that is in you with meekness and fear (respect).

I should mention that fear is used as two different definitions in the bible. One definition uses fear as respect or awe of God and the other is the usual definition as in scared or frightened. The reason of hope is because of God's love. I have been saved by grace and changed by God's Love. Hate, discrimination and condemnation doesn't help people want to change for the betterment of society. It changes people to the negative and dark side.

1 John 3:18 My little children, let us not love in word, neither in tongue; but in deed and in truth.

Our actions speak louder than words. The way we treat people matters more than what we say; although, kind words are helpful, too.

1 John 4:18 and 19 There is no fear in love; but perfect love casteth out fear because fear hath torment. He that feareth is not made perfect in love. (19) We love him, because he first loved us.

Homophobes are tormented. I speak from experience when I say that homophobes are usually closet gays. They are tormented inside themselves to be able to come out in a society that is hateful towards homosexuality. It is fear that prevents disclosure of self; and rightly so, with society's belief system based on the Old Testament traditions and punishment.

1 John 4:21 And this commandment have we from him; That he who loveth God love his brother also.

The commandment is love, not hate. The path in life becomes clearer when a personal relationship with God, Jesus and the Holy Spirit is developed and nurtured. It is the most important relationship in my life. That is why "GOD" is tattooed on my ring finger. When God is my priority, I can live with peace inside my own skin amongst all the chaos of this world.

VI. It's apparent that we can't rely on other people's interpretations of the bible if they are stuck in hate. That's why it's crucial to seek a personal relationship with God.

John 5:39 and 40 Search the scriptures; for in them ye think ye have eternal life; and they are thy which testify of me. (40) And ye will not come to me, that ye may have life.

Jesus says that the bible tells us stories from people that witnessed him. It is not what gives us what we need, though. Jesus gives us what we need. Many people can quote scripture, such as homophobes and the devil, but not have a clue of the truth of Jesus. They don't know him, only some fearful words written by scared witnesses in a book.

To know Jesus requires more than reading a book. It's just like a friendship with anyone else. We must spend time together, one on one, to communicate. We are supposed to incorporate the words of love from the bible into our hearts and display it by the use of our life. When those words and our actions match, it displays an honest, sane, peaceful life filled with Love. That is why much of this world seems insane… it's based on lies. Trying to make sense of lies drives a person crazy.

Matthew 7:7 and 8 Ask and it shall be given you; seek and ye shall find; knock and it shall be opened unto you; (8) For every one that asketh receiveth; and he that seeketh findeth; and to him that knocketh it shall be opened.

Jesus will meet you anytime, anywhere and under any circumstances. Get personal and he'll show you the truth.

Mark 7:33 And He took him aside from the multitude and put his fingers into his ears, and he spit, and touched his tongue.

Now that is up close and personal with Jesus. He did this to a man. I'll bet some people really freaked out about that. He is with us, inside of us and all around us. He is not far away, separate and distant. He is just waiting to be acknowledged.

John 15:3 Now ye are clean through the word which I have spoken unto you.

Jesus is the one that will speak to you and to your heart. It's hard to hear a message of love through anyone that hates and discriminates.

John 15:19 If ye were of the world, the world would love his own: but because ye are not of the world, but I have chosen you out of the world, therefore the world hateth you.

Those of us being persecuted for being different are the ones Jesus has chosen. Jesus goes to the oppressed. He chose GLBT people because we are being called outcasts, just like He was!

John 15:20 and 21 Remember the word that I have said unto you, the servant is not greater than his lord. If they have persecuted me, they will also persecute you; if they have kept my saying, they will keep yours also. (21) But all these things will they do unto you for my name's sake, because they know not him that sent me.

Jesus says it clearly here; that they are persecuting GLBT's just like they persecuted Him. It is also a way He lets us know that these people claiming their hateful actions are for Him are the false prophets.

John 16:13 Howbeit when he, the Spirit of truth is come, he will guide you into all truth: for he shall not speak of himself; but whatsoever he shall hear, that shall he speak: and he will shew you things to come.

Jesus is the truth. The truth shall set you free! His truth is love, not hate. His love will change you for the greater good.

John 16:33 These things I have spoken unto you that in me ye might have peace. In the world ye shall have tribulation: but be of good cheer; I have overcome the world.

Having a personal relationship with Jesus keeps the focus on love and peace. Homophobes want GLBT people to live in the tribulation, rather than the peace. Hang close to Jesus to overcome this world. Homophobes are tormented by their own sexual desires to be out and free.

John 20:29-31 Jesus saith unto him, "Thomas, because thou hast seen me, thou hast believed: blessed are they that have not seen, and yet have believed." (30) And many other signs truly did Jesus in the presence of his disciples, which are not written in this book. (31) But these are written, that ye might believe that Jesus is the Christ, the son of God; and that believing ye might have life through his name.

I write to bring new testimony of my life and my interpretation of the love Jesus has shown me. I speak of all the truth revealed to me so that I may heal and share this with the world. The last verse also tells us the bible is not complete. Jesus said those of us that believe but have not seen Him are blessed. Our testimony is even more powerful!

Acts 18:9-10 Then spake the Lord to Paul in the night by a vision, "Be not afraid, but speak, and hold not thy peace; (10) For I am with thee, and no man shall set on thee to hurt thee: for I have much people in this city."

Jesus says don't keep the peace by hiding the truth out of fear from homophobic bullies. Speak out to help self and others that are suffering.

Romans 2:19 And art confident that thou thyself art a guide of the blind, a light of them which are in darkness.

I am claiming Jesus' love, truth and guidance for writing all of this about acceptance for all. Especially GLBT's being targeted based on people's interpretations of the bible. My interpretation is based on personal experience and relations with Christ. And I am chosen to bring this to light. If I don't share this testimony, I am just as bad as those that are being hateful. As the verse reads, I can't be afraid to speak out on this issue.

Romans 12:2 And be not conformed to this world: but be ye transformed by the renewing of your mind, that ye may prove what is good, and acceptable, and perfect, will of God.

We GLBT's do not have to conform to the old ways and old ideas to believe and have Christ in our lives. We get transformed by Jesus' Love when we engage in a personal relationship with Him. He will teach that there is no room for hate and no place for any human being to bash another.

All of chapter 12 in Romans is awesome. It points out our different gifts according to grace and our oneness in Christ. Our own conscience is to be our guide. When we are in tune with Jesus' Love, we will be more loving, kind, merciful and giving. We will not want to be hateful to anyone.

Romans 16:20 And the God of peace shall bruise Satan under your feet shortly. The grace of our Lord Jesus Christ be with you. Amen

It reads the God of Peace, not hate. Satan is hate.

2 Corinthians 12:9 And he said unto me, "My grace is sufficient for thee: for my strength is made perfect in weakness." Most gladly therefore will I rather glory in my infirmities, that the power of Christ may rest upon me.

My problems or weaknesses brought me to Jesus. He gives me strength to walk in truth. I can be grateful for the problems because they remind me to go to Jesus for strength. I am not alone. I used to be held back from a relationship with God, Jesus and the Holy Spirit because I believed the lies from the Old Testament that were forced down my throat. Now knowing that those lies are not what God intended, I am FREE to seek the truth brought by Jesus Christ. I now have a very powerful personal relationship with God, Jesus and the Holy Spirit.

Galatians 6:15 and 16 For in Christ Jesus neither circumcision availeth anything, nor uncircumcision but a new creature. (16) And as many as walk according to this rule, peace be on them, and mercy, and upon the Israel of God.

Jesus doesn't discriminate gay or straight. Those that live by that, walk in peace and mercy.

Ephesians 2:11-22 (UNITED AND EQUAL IN CHRIST!!!) Wherefore remember that ye being in time past Gentiles in the flesh, who are called uncircumcision by that which is called the circumcision in the flesh made by hands; (12) That at that time ye were without Christ being aliens from the commonwealth of Israel, and strangers from the covenants of promise, having no hope and without God in the world: (13) But now in Christ Jesus ye who sometimes were far off are made nigh (near) by the blood of Christ. (14) For he is our peace, who hath made both one, and hath broken down the middle wall of partition between us; (15) Having abolished in his flesh the enmity (active hatred) even the law of commandments contained in ordinances; for to make in himself of twain one new man, so making peace; (16) And that he might reconcile both unto God in one body by the cross, having slain the enmity thereby; (17) And came and preached peace to you which were afar off, and to them that were nigh. (18) For through him we both have access by one Spirit unto the Father. (19) Now therefore ye are no more strangers and foreigners, but fellowcitizens with the saints, and of the household of God; (20) And are built upon the foundation of the apostles and prophets, Jesus Christ himself being the chief cornerstone; (21) In whom all the building fitly framed together growth unto an holy temple in the Lord: (22) In whom ye also are builded together for an habitation of God through the Spirit.

Verses 15 and 16 say that Jesus got rid of the enmity, active hatred, and law of commandments in his flesh. His crucifixion was to release us from the old traditions of condemnation and punishment. Anyone still practicing active hatred is NOT in Christ!!! Christians or anyone else that tries to use the bible for gay bashing are liars.

Philippians 4:6-9 Be careful for nothing; but in everything by prayer and supplication with thanksgiving let your requests be made known unto God. (7) And the peace of God, which passeth all understanding, shall keep your hearts and minds through Christ Jesus. (8) Finally brethren, whatsoever things are true, whatsoever things are honest, whatsoever things are just, whatsoever things are pure, whatsoever things are lovely, whatsoever things are of good report; if there be any virtue, and if there be any praise, think on these things. (9) Those things, which ye have both learned, and received, and heard, and seen in me, do: and the God of peace shall be with you.

Life of peace comes from living Jesus' words of love. Life of chaos comes from hate.

Colossians 3:11 Where there is neither Greek nor Jew, circumcision nor uncircumcision, Barbarian, Scythian, bond nor free: but Christ is all, and in all.

Jesus doesn't discriminate. Anyone that wants to get personal with Him is welcome.

1 Thessalonians 5:5 Ye are the children of light, and the children of the day: we are not of the night, nor of darkness.

Hatred and discrimination are darkness.

1 Timothy 4:16 Take heed unto thyself, and unto the doctrine; continue in them: for in doing this thou shalt both save thyself, and them that hear thee.

Pass along the good news… JESUS LOVES GAYS, LESBIANS, BI-SEXUALS AND TRANSGENDERS!

Hebrews 10:36 and 38 For ye have need of patience, that after ye have done the will of God, ye might receive the promise. (38) Now the just shall live by faith: but if any man drawback, my soul shall have no pleasure in him.

God's promises come true when living a life based on love and tolerance that Jesus teaches.

1 Peter 2:1-4 Wherefore laying aside all malice, and all guile, and hypocrisies, and envies, and all evil speaking, (2) As newborn babes desire the sincere milk of the word, that ye may grow thereby: (3) If so be ye have tasted that the Lord is gracious. (4) To whom coming, as unto a living stone, disallowed indeed of men, but chosen of God, and precious.

Sincerely trying to do God's will and trying to live by the principle of Love brings peace inside my body and mind. My Spirit is solid because it is God.

1 Peter 3:16 Having a good conscience; that whereas they speak evil of you, as of evildoers, they may be ashamed that falsely accuse your good conversation in Christ.

People will try to tear you down when you speak freely of Christ's Love and Truth. But you will have a clear and clean conscience and Peace inside your heart. Seek a personal relationship with Jesus through quiet time of prayer and meditation. He'll also help you to know and distinguish between the truth, false prophets and who to believe.

VII. God, Jesus and the Holy Spirit will show the true from false in a variety of ways.

Luke 10:21 In that hour Jesus rejoiced in spirit, and said, I thank thee, O Father Lord of heaven and earth, that thou hast hid these things from the wise and prudent, and hast revealed them unto babes: even so, Father; for so it seemed good in thy sight.

Jesus is referring to the powers given to new and genuine believers called babes. These powers are kept from the wise and prudent so as to not be abused. The babes are sincere to spread the truth of Jesus about love and equality. Our political system and religions are full of examples of what happens when the powers are in the wrong hands. There are extreme cases of discrimination and crimes against GLBT's. There are people with power to stop the oppression but don't.

James 2:19 Thou believe that there is one God; thou doest well: the devils also believe and tremble.

I have love and peace of mind, not fear and trembling, because of my belief in God.

Romans 10:13-15 For whosoever shall call upon the name of the Lord shall be saved. (14) How then shall they call on him in whom they have not believed? And how shall they believe in him of whom they have not heard? And how shall they hear without a preacher? (15) And how shall they preach except be sent? As it is written, How beautiful are the feet of them that preach the gospel of peace, and bring glad tidings of good things.

Here's an easy way to tell a false prophet: are they teaching and preaching peace and love or hate and discriminate? Are they stuck in the Old Testament or into Jesus' Truth of the New Testament?

Romans 16:17 and 18 Now I beseech you, brethren, mark them which cause divisions and offenses contrary to the doctrine which ye have learned; and avoid them. (18) For they that are such serve not our Lord Jesus Christ, but their own belly; and by good works and fair speeches deceive the hearts of the simple.

These verses are powerful examples of a false prophet. If people are being divisive, such as discriminating and excluding a minority group, and are not teaching Jesus' love, then they are false prophets.

James 3:17 and 18 But the wisdom that is from above is first pure, then peaceable, gentle, and easy to be intreated, full of mercy and good fruits, without partiality, and without hypocrisy. (18)And the fruit of righteousness is sown in peace of them that make peace.

God makes it so easy to tell who is a false prophet. Are they sowing peace or spewing hate?

Colossians 1:21 and 22 And you, that were sometimes alienated and enemies in your own mind by wicked works, yet now hath he reconciled. (22) In the body of his flesh through death, to present you holy and unblameable and unreproveable in his sight.

When we stop believing the lies from the false prophets, and build a personal relationship with Jesus, we will grow in the understanding that we are holy and loved! No matter whom we are and what we've done, Jesus loves us. Nail all the negativity to His cross and leave it there. He's got it covered. We are forgiven.

Romans 8:16 and 17 The Spirit itself bear witness with one Spirit that we are the children of God; And if children, then heirs; heirs of God and joint heirs with Christ if so be that we suffer with him that we may be also glorified together.

We are HOLY in and with Christ as believers in Jesus. We suffer with him as being crucified for our differences.

Galatians 5:4 Christ is become of no effect unto you whosoever of you are justified by the law; ye are fallen from grace.

Those of you that try to use Moses' law to bash gays have proven Christ is not in you. There is no grace in hate. It's easy to spot a false prophet. Homophobes that claim Jesus' name to discriminate are some of them.

Ephesians 6:12 we wrestle against spiritual wickedness in high places…

Using money, power and Christ's name to discriminate against GLBT people is spiritual wickedness.

1 Peter 1:15 But as he which hath called you is holy, so be ye holy in all manner of conversation.

We are God's kids… HOLY and LOVED!!!

1 Peter 1:16 Be holy, for I am holy.

Believe that you are holy because you are a child of God. Anyone that believes is.

1 Thessalonians 4:8 and 11 He therefore that despiseth, despiseth not man, but God, who hath also given unto us his holy spirit. (11) And that ye study to be quiet, and to do your own business, and to work with your own hands, as we commanded you…

People need to mind their own business and live their own lives instead of focusing on the lives of GLBT people. Live and let live.

1 Peter 4:12 and 13 Beloved, think it not strange concerning the fiery trial which is to try you, as though some strange thing happened unto you. (13) But rejoice, inasmuch as ye are partakers of Christ's sufferings; that when his glory shall be revealed, ye may be glad also with exceeding joy.

GLBT people are suffering from people's ignorance, just like Jesus suffered for being different than their traditional standards.

Hebrews 9:14 How much more shall the blood of Christ, who through the eternal Spirit offered himself without spot to God, purge your own conscience from dead works to serve the living God?

What more proof do we need that God loves us and wants greater things for us? The blood of Jesus is to wash away ALL past mistakes to give us a fresh start. Dead works are those old ideas from the Old Testament. Those traditions must be replaced by Jesus' teachings of Love. The dead works are the ideas that keep people stuck in the crucifixion period and prevent people from discovering the new works of the resurrection. That's where being 'born again' offers us the new life with Jesus… arise and walk freely into a new, beautiful, loved filled life.

Luke 21:12-19 But before all these, they shall lay their hands on you, and persecute you, delivering you up to the synagogues, and into prisons, being brought before kings and rulers for my names sake, (13) And it shall turn to you for a testimony (14) Settle it therefore in your hearts, not to meditate before what ye shall answer: (15) For I will give you a mouth and wisdom which all your adversaries shall not be able to gainsay nor resist (16) And ye shall be betrayed both by parents, and brethren, and kinsfolks, and friends, and some of you shall they cause to be put to death (17) And ye shall be hated of all men for my name's sake (18) But there shall not an hair of your head perish (19) In your patience possess ye your souls.

WOW! ...very powerful! Jesus says we that believe in Him will be at home in our own skin even while we are being rejected and persecuted by all that are supposed to love us. How many of you have been rejected by your own family and friends because of being gay, lesbian, bi-sexual or transgender? I have. That was a very lonely place to be. It helped push me to Jesus, though. When my relationship with Jesus developed to the level and strength it is now, I remain filled with God's Love even when it feels like no one else loves me! God, Jesus and the Holy Spirit will never abandon me… or you.

The people that say God hates GLBT people do NOT know God. The authorities that spew hatred do NOT know Jesus. Many only study the words in the bible, but don't develop a personal relationship with Jesus. Those that know the words and use them to oppress anyone certainly don't know Christ!!! Those that do not follow Jesus' path of love and mercy and use His name against us are the homophobes trying to keep us down.

There is a huge difference between reading the bible, studying it and applying it into one's life. I have read the "King James" version of the New Testament. That has the teachings of Jesus Christ which is truly all about the LOVE! I hope you will turn to the loving Jesus that I have described for the beautiful life He offers us here and now.

Please don't let the longstanding lies of the old ideas in the Old Testament keep you from seeking an extraordinary personal relationship with Jesus Christ. I plan to disclose my path to the inner peace I have found through Christ in my next writings. All the details that led me to the cross and become Spirit Led will show you that if I could get there, so can you! Blessings to all.

PEACE & LOVE

References:

1.) The "King James" version of the New Testament

2.) Merriam Webster's Collegiate Dictionary 10th Edition

Printed in Great Britain
by Amazon